The Grand Reopening

The Grand Reopening

Toby Davidson

Puncher & Wattmann

First published in 2025
Published by Puncher & Wattmann
PO Box 279
Waratah NSW 2298

info@puncherandwattmann.com

A catologue record for this book is available from The National Library of Australia.

ISBN 9781923099616

Cover design by David Musgrave

Cover photograph by Toby Davidson

Printed by Lightning Source International

Contents

Fable for Erin

From a dawning outcrop
by the sea
rose All-to-come
and All-to-be.

When the world
had lost its head,
two present tenses
went to bed.

When the world
had found its tongue,
the outcrop by the sea
was gone.

All-to-come
and All-to-be
still spiral, hunt
this century.

An Octopus Tests My Left Big Toe

Freaking twice, in real life by a grey-green beauty
with sapphire eyes;
their rockpool laboratory ankle-deep under a headland
in a state of collapse.

At the second tap-tap, hypotheses ninefold swirled
in feverish sand. Listen yet –
Observe how the curio moans, withdraws, symptomatic
of a nervous central brain.

In clarity's way, the sun's dark twin. Tentacles, anyone?
Tease what you can…
Even I, akimbo in a world of wind, see octoprotocols
urge retreat, cometlike,

to a seasnail-splattered rim. There, in the pink-green
crackling dissonance,
elite concentration with no field report – just a bustling
cloud of nine minds to run

rings around, bar a weedy lair, or swat subconscious fish
and share from a sand-wall
the last and first sapphire test. My heartbeat cavorts
like a satisfied philistine.

Temporal Disintegration Love Poem

Is love the blood of the universe?
The Log Lady, *Twin Peaks*

Love, the stupefied days run together, are marked before they reach us. We keep and lose track, change clothes, re-adapt. It's all we've got to go on.

Love, state-sanctioned fugue states never slow so much as soften; we'll have to get used to each other like this. Wine night is a yes and a cure for prediction. Each of the speeds we can't see are still there.

Love, in your loading screens my resting face is fear. But if we finish *Twin Peaks*, are you darting through pines, squawking backwards, snapping at flesh-folds of mist?

Love, float closer in a Newport seabath, mischievous sun-struck glint on your cheek. I try survival backstroke for its jellyfish laziness, reach back for concrete and scrape my left wrist. White-bellied crabs in the corner drain flinch, return to their slime soon, according to the water.

Love, are we both meant to be at work? Bungan Head dodged a microburst tornado three or four daily briefings back. Lord, the hostage negotiations, inner sanctums...

Love, your glib immunity just ate the sun, now you're really showing off. It's warped to be aging in sight of this, especially now birthdays are dead, if we're honest, for adults, and aging's not current but twice as annihilating and is likewise showing off.

Love, if we float belly-up (not the dead man's), the stinging corners of our eyes make two vanishing points of the same collapsing star down to the atom of time we fell out of. And on to thoughts of dinner.

Love, you were there, throughout weightlessness and weight, fierce as the rocking mirror itself, the face you radiate when you don't really have to. No one's fickle (as distinct from arbitrary), not even the big daddy of passable gasping, not even the sheep's blood delivered to my door.

Love, disintegrating in you was relief when we were hard-headed and time-poor. Let's make our ways, distress or mend some. It's just not the night to take us home, save for more futureless monitoring.

Tyranny

We had our houses too, though nobody believes us… They were about 4 feet (1.2 metres) high, with stones and heavy boughs. Each one would be covered with leaves and dirt to make a watertight roof… you'd put [animal] skin over it on a cold night if the fire wasn't going… When the smallpox hit everyone crawled inside because they had fevers and that, and all these things were just full of bodies. It was easy for the redcoats to come along and torch them. Don't forget we're talking about hundreds and hundreds of bodies; the stench must have been phenomenal.

Gai-mariagal man Dennis Foley in Foley and Peter Read, *What the Colonists Never Knew: A History of Aboriginal Sydney*

Passing strange muster, no limits to who plain chokes;
the similar here out-teaches the same,
makes blows of its points and points of its blows…
The bushfires cleared to this transparent horror,
this ravenous sea with erasure-rich air
of land reclaimed, family time swallowed.
Tyranny! The tellie shrieks. *They've all lost our votes.*
The sickos in power are seriously enjoying this.
Christmas is lost… We live in a police state!
Who gave them permission to target our families?
What gives them the right to decide where I go?
I meant in no way to diminish the Holocaust.

To 'It's a free country', add asterisk, asterisk;
so rip off the cape and sit down where we are.
I read, walled away from the Avalon Cluster,
how Gai-mariagal men smoke Avalon caves
to coax out spirits of their smallpox dead
who still can't be swayed to move on.
How those who evaded the cruel spotted skin
– mark of the Crown, make it look like an accident –

exhaled the reek of their homes on the wind,
(en)countered a language with thralldom for them
in its outbreak, variants, chains of transmission
by murder and rape, by decree and kidnapping
forever from places of burning concern.

We're cut off now, Dennis, at the heart of your world,
Narrabeen, where *carang* doze on feathery lamplids
reddened by dawn from today's dose of memory.
Or maybe they're gone, or aren't fishily subject to
Area Command's presence-absence at the Neck,
their beaks hiding more than their bellies can…
Tyranny! Un-Australian! Bronzed tatts and flags
with a British return-stamp and asterisk rile me,
but I'm of the 'sheeple' they don't mean as heirs
to that gated invasive species, mind. (*Gag*).
Crank conspiracies run interference for the blatant ones
and no one's leaving Sydney's pristine Northern Beaches.

Resurfacing, Newport

A whale's worth of whitewater
spikes in the glare
of the bay, won't fade

but drifts – on my
life – through
the teeth of the wind

into quarrelling shades
robed in sparks,
trailing nothing new.

Propelled to the end,
they are assumed
and are comprised

to compromise
and peel away from
their own suspension

back to the tonnes
and fins constellated
to upset the overblown sun.

Haircuts and Happy Hour

The news has flipped out... Here's a line at a hairdresser,
queue at a pub (where they also cut hair). *We now cross live*
to a mother of five with prosecco in an upscale salon...

Re-entering means re-entertaining the Real World, a strange
kind of panic no one ever really masters. La Niña storms
in gunmetal humidity; a sour haunting shows it knows

its way around us. We learn to avoid people physically again,
bob and spin like hallway balloons, the swoosh of space-time
rearranging around us like gloop for the sanitised ten.

We're intemperate water, hence the lack of surrender.
Hence horses, choppers, the Great Resignation, roadblocks, hidden
choirs. Hence working from work in a staged release, students

instinctively spaced down a corridor to rush dust's imposters
from sanctified seats. Of thirty plus, half have impeccable hair;
the remains of their faces temp-scanned, happy and scared.

The Point of Theatre

A pregnant pause on opening night
alive with doubt

is nothing now, but at the time
in gaping dark,

hair we never knew we had
stood on end

with a crackling violence
of animal reliance,

this once worth
going out for.

Return to the Hotel Steyne

The beer tastes as good as avoiding the present,
regenerating social cues, scratching my head
in three-sixty degrees. Is this careless, is it care?
I'll raise the wrist on a need-to-know-basis
and elbow-bump fairy-lit ninjas like me,
our dancefloor denuded of accents and tans.

My voice feels scratchy by nine and no convo
can shake itself free from the saved and irretrievable.
Scull, cut loose! Is it careless, is it care?
The past can strike out in a roped-off area,
bouncers kick an old salt out in real time
and I choke in the ping pong final to grief

from the threadbare crowd – too Anglo, too male –
then it's back to the taps with my consolation
tenner, where I'm pinned and at the mercy
of a maggot close-talker and remotely
fantasise I'm handing over for his murder.

For the Suffering

An abyss is just that, an abyss.
I would say *At least* to the abyss
or *Kiss this*; I would say it's remiss
of my people to frequent our lives
like abysses thought to stop and didn't
have lives of their own antimatter
edging round us just as much,
trying not to fall in. They take
and negate with an animal heart
like it's meant to be deep, some kind
of sick comfort when they're out there,
actually actually in byss-ness,
eating my people with insidious mists.

We now know the price
of a rickety bridge built from
other abysses, the only way over.
We're born for this, cross
with antimatter in our wake,
but abysses trail in packs,
schoolgirl-giddy with their claims.
Their eyes stare back, meet ours
of stinging blood, piss themselves,
wake screaming in their juices
and know how we burned through
the dark before A led to B.

The first cradle rocked, then,
was over abysses, first shoulder
wept on, smeared dreamlike walls,
first reddened faces all failing
at wrongness, the actual actual wrongness

which snarls around the heartsick.
Abysses don't swallow themselves
like us. Pity. (Their rickety
bridges to date null and void.)
My lovelies, should agony/agonies hear us,
may they stay home, grief-torn
by disembodiment, emptied for real
by the weight of their hunger.

And stuff them. Right to their fabled depths.
Take all they have
and turn them human in revenge.

Gymea Lilies

Pungent afterthoughts
of power, star-encrusted streets.

At the core of the rainstorm,
the heart of the flower.

Your highnesses
clump like scruffy planets.

Erupt, secrete
at the jesting distance.

Off My Face and Skin at the Dentist

'Have you had nitrous oxide?'   I gurgle, re-widen
think *Not since the 90s*   *Bring your acid back on*
but it's 9am and dentistry   is the scene
with laughing gas primed   and face-shielded Leanne
who wounds instrumentally   hovers like a seraph.
Her hygienist lowers   a polymer mask
with a dangling tube and   faint flow. I sink from sight
in the padded chair   for a flatscreen live on the ceiling.
'Georgia, turn down the   nitrous.' It's working, they're
working beneath *Planet Earth*   in my orbit, sublime.
My pulse is racing   Earth's hues swarm and beat
like the creatures they live in   and that's a nice thought
wreathed in light…   I shut my eyes to a hot 90s rave.

Georgia vacuums, cranes.   Leanne injects some local.
'Did you catch that clip   of the pod down at Manly?
Are the visuals ok?   I love *Planet Earth*.'
Leanne's cheeks crease   and I sense I'm snake!
She wilts psychotropically   and I sense I'm a snake
with a world-eating maw   astronomically detached
fangs sunk in an egg   which is Earth, yet expands
til we're stuck mid-dance   between hunter and prey
the atmosphere between us   holding sway, holding sway…
'Susan, turn up the nitrous.   You'll say if there's pain?
I'll wash away the taste.'   Now Susan? What of Georgia,
her character arc?   My heart pumps diagonally.
Tears surprise. Gulp.   'Plenty more where that came from.'

The chased get away   with divine orchestration.
Sir David insists on a human   voice. (That I'm
a snake neither here   nor there, jawing
his radiant world-egg.)   Instruments hiss and coil

surreal as hot streams   down the face of a snake.
In the jungle, competition   for food is intense.
The transformed male   attempts a display!
I could still insist   on a human voice
but I'm cut loose   into chiming air
absurdly drooling   as the street competes
with a satellite view   of this green-blue egg
in my upscaled head   I could yet mark for prey.
And I longed to again   lock my teeth around the Earth…

Lyric Past the Hard Border

Pines creak in formation,
keep it down to a dull roar.

Their crow-calls are are
arrrrrrrrreee blue sun.

A loveliness breaks
back and forth

to contain itself,
trailing crackling salt.

The Doctor and
fishscale surface shine

muss the crowns
of the amber-eyed,

who glare magisterially,
each pompous stride

sending up
our intrinsic

surviving
preposterousness.

Inescapable Airport Love Poem

It is very sweet to wander lost in love
Along the desolate ways Love makes us travel.
Hadewijch of Brabant, 'Becoming Love with Love'

Love, everyone knows purgatory is an airport, but we'll trade purgatories up to a point.

Love, everyone *buys* there's something to be said for assuming former purgatories, but no one admits it.

Love, it's in the way they welcome you back: in minutes you're trapped, detached and enduring some neutral gate to turn portal of old, without the years departed.

Love, remember how duty free mocked us, how the corridors in and out are the same? Flights land, but transfer us only in a dead heat, our last dangling slice of wherewithal.

Love, the whole caper is maniacally clean. We loop back on ourselves with soul-crushing panache, but we've got squat on the hosties and captains with gold-embossed shoulders who gleam past unerringly, paying no mind and paying for nothing, wheels and heels in attack formation.

Love, how can anyone know what's deserved? The gates keep changing with numbers, bodies, toilets. Officials and cleaners keep charmlessly holy the same antiseptic disregard.

Love, scan this, stick your arms out and listen. Don't let despair ground you down or play co-pilot. *Run, don't walk, to your next appointment*, announcements ring with a sealed-in tone. We cling to the base illusion of ascent.

Love, they've perfected the tech to upgrade souls! You'd have a time of it, don't have me on – the few who never perished from you upgraded to platinum class in the members' lounge with all the shiny wine.

Love, we'll trade purgatories up to a point we thought we'd decide in all fairness. So what? Why rage to a toddler's defeat at the exits, miss crisps, drinks, friends, ecstasies of torched cloud, decay and make-up in a better light, this month's new releases?

The Gull-Cries of Dublin

Steadfast, the size of sleek chickens by the Liffey,
they gather on ledges, in parks beside pigeons,
cranes, ducks, tramping voices, abrupt sodden craics.

These gulls hold back, far more self-contained
than their scrappy, red-beaked Antipodean derivatives.
They're not predisposed to tear anything apart.

It's like they've been let in on something else.
Impassive eyes narrow, comply and hide news.
In flight, they'll admit to an eagle's bearing,

concentric brown patterns the span of the young.
As earthly merriment wanes to blue nothing
and Grafton Street cools, pubs, bins spill again,

and over its vagrancies, the *Ee-ee-ee-ees*
of sonic sentries, juveniles higher-pitched,
braid rainstreaked alleys to pre-Viking banks.

Who goes there now in what passes for the still?
They pry and repel uncontactable chill
from ruffled flesh with the blackest keening.

The Sistine Chapel

Beneath the Creator's reach, the Golden Ratio
of tourist thrum stirs guards to the mike.
Silenzio. Silence. No photo. No video.

Wonder at what ate the eyes of Michelangelo;
anciently capture a spreading dark
beneath the Creator's reach, the Golden Ratio

breathed into brushstrokes of *immagini di Dio.*
The roof is eternity, tongues slowly spike.
Silenzio. Silence. No photo. No video.

This century's guests, from Beijing to Rio,
quell themselves by Christ's raised hand, snake
beneath the Creator's reach, the Golden Ratio

pinched from nature's windings. The cameo
of a fleshless selfie on a flayed saint strikes.
Silenzio. Silence. No photo. No video.

Adam sighs. Your stretch of time finito,
you can't take with you as much as you'd like.
Beneath the Creator's reach, the Golden Ratio,
nessun silenzio. No silence. Photo. Video.

Floating Over Atlantis

The tour boat hums from the red cliffs of Oia
to obsidian mounds with a milkier turquoise
splishing their rust-coloured rims. There's fear about
in this Aegean Mordor that last blew its stack
post the Greek Civil War. Thera well back, Santorini
the remains from fireballs and ash of 1600 BCE
when nothing would grow and the sea ate a kingdom
for hubris and greed and their own elevation.
Olympus dispatched thus these artful impersonators,
courters of beauty unlikely to sacrifice
deigned to become what it means with their bodies:
a message to trouble the blessed and exceptional,
alone in its splitting of crust and human ears,
four times the billowing rage of Krakatoa.
The Atlantis pretext wasn't lost on Plato, Verne:
the wicked commended to silence beneath them,
cremated by raised ancient blood.
It's swimmable. Sulphurous though. Leaves a stain.
I roll on my back, which disconcerts no fish
in patches of warmth reminiscent of piss
and metallic tartness shared on the tongue
by Brits, Yanks, Italians intermingled with laughter
captured, uploaded and vented – *That's fire!* –
as we ease into, tease the caldera of punishment,
in love with ourselves, floating over Atlantis.

Relocations

So that's where the salt is, can't find a charger,
but most of our flat has survived unobserved.

A balcony succulent roared to red flower
infused with the boisterous sea and for weeks

was a god of sorts, now caught in the act
which has at its heart immanence and exposure.

We sheepishly greet, extend our extravagances,
humbled a little by the pearl afternoon;

me and this replicating little desert genius
we'll heal with, eat and envy in imperishable Space.

Livestreamed Funerals

Words, by weight of numbers, *do.*
Burnt ones curl and elevate.
The insufficiency the same, resistance –
but death is a jealous distance
pushing us into the frame regardless,
bonding or branching down
each remote face. We're physically
drawn to the generous still,
despite winning, which pales
before loss when it's not a game.
The family rise in parts and together,
to music and of it. Their tremor
speaks louder. We cover
our mouths in grey studies.

Sunday After Five

I can't claim too much,
as too much
nearly happened.

A late set too much
for a young
teenage girl.

The sea floor too much
fell away,
disarranged her.

Her black hair too much
was thrown
over her cries.

Her friend yelled too much
when a scream
would have done.

Chest-deep, too much
in my head
to break, dolphin,

I wallowed too much
til I caught
her friend's eyes.

*

She was too much
in shock
to raise a stroke.

She didn't have too much
left towards
the heavens.

Her face was too much
of a black veil
to hear me.

I swept too much
of her hair
from her death

for it to stay too much
longer than foam.
We'll both breathe.

Her tongue, too, much
gone until
the shallows.

The Emergency Declared Over, May '23

I

The emergency has mutated back to a threat. It's still with us, stalking the frail like the flu. Keep your shots up for winter, a summer or two without megafires and you're right as rain til it floods. If you don't laugh you'll cry or move to a town where chastising parrots screech between powerlines as rain crashes in, both bitter and fresh to the same supposed tongue. It's riskier *not* to inhale.

II

For Dad, in pretty good nick but over eighty, it wasn't *hellish.* 'Not for you!' snorts Mum down the line. 'There I was, Florence Nightingale, up and down stairs all night despite the injection in my ankle.' I'm first to break: 'Tough crowd, Dad!' 'Don't I know it', he closes the loop in mock-outrage. 'Annnyway…' Not sure the source, revealed by a RAT test, we push it down and away in our minds. To the lexicon, add 'antivirals'.

III

I'm searching for continuity here. Love is greater than death, not because of Love's deathlessness, but this: even Love is unsure if we made it up. And it created everything.

IV

Bat, pangolin, raccoon dog, secret scientist? Seven million gone, three years flung into the void. We iron hems which semi-fit, recover unjustified outings, break the unspoken pact to roam unmarked and stay the lonely hell away from wishing for contact which can't be replaced and don't dwell, don't stop now to think of them grainily. Friends, or what-have-you, save yourselves!

V

On this day, I confess to nothing but ignorance as to my own co-morbidities under the eyes and assumptions of the State. I can offer a Syndrome, by name Klippel-Trenaunay, but will the first strain to breach me be stunned to find another at large on the throne of my biology? *You can't have him*, I want KTS to hiss, but I'm just one voice in the warm, swollen stream that hears only inversion, compression, or the surgeon. Its venous ear is tuned to green-red gravity, port-wine stain hip to toe, a polyphonic revolt under threat of incompetence easy to blame on the valves, the vowels, the vows which won't let a word in and come with the territory. Write, writhe, write.

Primordial Mist on Mooney Mooney Bridge

This blazing day has all the answers, down to a leaf-edge
ultradefined, to a thicket of arm hair tensed
against the steering wheel, shadow-script crawling
to the line of the sun. A blowfly's wing casts
a minor masterpiece from my clamped wiper blade
at a hundred and ten: segmentation, fragmentation,
the works. Is its body beneath? Ridgelines
sag like fire, the kind with duelling demands.

The canyon colossal now, down to the creek.
Air floats sweet and is river already under six lanes
of twin cantilevered bridge, 'The Big Dipper'
(1986, Hawkie cut the cord). It's pure motorist myth
where the scarred rock sinks, superstructure
at the guts engulfed faintly with its cars,
with a parapet fence reinforced after seventeen years
of unbelted, pulled-over flying bodies…

My vehicle levels, percussive at speed;
two tawny wind-socks mark the last of the seen
by a river of mist at cross-purposes to concrete,
to filthy trucks as to impeccable sky. We're now
ploughing into this dawn-of-time remnant
with flesh-metal shudderings   gold strands
for feelers   omnipresent-absent   and loving it
minus the finest   wisp of regret
        (fine)   (fin)   (in)   (i)

Same heart. Hang on to air-kissing oblivion
in the uncertain, where we most have it wrong:
it's not just relief from others' tauntings,
but closing on everything in the unseen,

where you still have a body but nothing else does,
with the need for nothing supreme (or the gist).
Pain, rancour conk out here. What matters is drizzling,
elated, implied: vision is void while an ego loss of mist
tears strips from these godlike mornings, limits, wings.

All One Breath

I Fig Leaves

Caught between kiss and abyss
since the day, this pair
(withered? ripe?) have declined
every interview, quaking
and whispering inward instead,
a touch – it can't stand
unsaid – pathologically.

II Ugly People at the Beach

In the end it's interior,
the sea teaches that, far away
from what hotness looks out for,
removes, from slavering froth
to the pressurised trenches
where eyes are for fools
and for lunch like the sun.

III Windfarms from a Plane

Precisely staggered shock-white
graveyards of the half-boiled sea
pinpoint survival through
clouds' bottom lines
extracted and charred,
tormenting every temperature –
we, in turn, burn to descend.

IV Today's Simile

Like a stolen car on the Harbour
Bridge – ablaze, upturned
in Cretaceous morning mist –
disaster adores us
written off with a twist
as part of a larger
swoonworthy, gripping arc.

V Doornail Surprise

I'm yet unsure how a drowned cicada,
taken in for its crimson eyes
and gothic wings,
bashed about the sink
a full two days on and clung,
vibrating, to the flimsy bark-strip
lowered at a loss to drag it out.

VI Grip

There are sorrows
that swallow words whole
and I've heard them
cooly choke torn-up types
who would otherwise
speak, but 'otherwise'
belongs to sorrow.

VII Sleep is Already the Infinite

No one sees the full array
of breath and pain
which gave time pause
and even held it twice
at sea on flickering lids
in pillowy greys, just quietly
real and unbelievable.

Rescue

I hang out with what I suppose is your ghost
and call you by only the last of your names,
I in my new place and you in yours.
It's waggling bliss before recall and what took you
snarl in combined from the teeth of an ocean
too broad to tear around, comical hound.
My ears prick up at your claw-on-lino patter
complete with the crash of a flyscreen door.
Your shape's reassertions, stir-crazy with breeze,
run with the glossy-coated spirit of play
finding your fur which can't be contained.
Envious glints at the window pant and paw.
You lick, I lose touch with our stray afternoons,
your mind to return. You've come from nowhere before.

The King Parrots See to It

With love if possible and with force if necessary.
Benito Mussolini

A century past the March on Rome for Ol' Boulderhead,
fascism preens itself alive again.
Winter rain thins on a mountainside suburb,
black cloak thrown over the skittish sun.

A model of perfection, me, fascism gushes.
Blame, victimhood never get old or less libidinous.
A clutch of king parrots, young males orange-
breasted, bind the chill in deep shrieking knots.

As if Boulderhead's pals and spies and wealth
might cease to exist, sheer greed denied a passport!
King parrots chitter, parade along a palm-leaf;
a fourth shoots clean into my neighbour's window.

Ashen-mouthed children from the war of wars
can't match the absence of recall, mass shuddering.
The fourth king parrot, surprised by a limit (wham!)
falters mid-air, scythes away to a brimming gum.

Send off the clowns – Meloni, Bibi, Trump and Vlad –
from a plot of forced love for Mad William, unceded.
Rain down a boulder dislodged from the caves.
King parrots occupy me now until it crashes in.

Straya Quartet

I Just Another Aussie Nazi

My first Aussie Nazi was Jack van Tongeren,
Perth's wannabe cosplay Hitler of the Hills.
He shared a bunker, regalia and doctrine
with his followers, flags and slurs and drills,
hot-blooded copiers hectic with posters screaming
'Racial War!' and how to fear Jews and Asians.
Jack went down in '89 for firebombing
Chinese restaurants on four occasions.
Once, boys my age snorted Nazis weren't us,
but wound-up sweaty German klutzes
dispatched by Indiana Jones into ravines
to cries of *Scheisse!* or the Wilhelm Scream.
And now today's tattooed enforcer in a blue sedan
is van Tongeren of The Entrance Road on Darkinjung land…

II The AFG, Popular as Ever

The Ahistorical Fair Go wakes in a cabbage patch
with dulled memories of the night before.
Something rough in relation to war once a year?

The AFG sways to its feet and its fellows
are rousing as one from their cabbage beds, the same.
They declare *We must be equal and fair,*

for indeed the sun is breaking out to light the way!
It's thrilling to speak, almost like an escape,
and the cabbage folk call themselves blessed

or distressed to the core and get sick of it, sick
at those elements taking a shot at their knockabout harvest.
They work hard at everything other than this.

III The National Pastime

It doesn't have an off-season.
It's not abandoned due to rain
and can't be overcome by heat.
Class and race determine only
who stays in the news.

It's solitary or family-oriented.
Thousands don't sense
how they even take part in it;
thousands who shouldn't know,
know that they do – tiniest
vessels for such untender rage.

What shows is a tell: hells
where men throw control around,
love/have to win
in the national pastime,
conceive of what else
but putting women in the ground.

IV The Captains of Fear

The tabloid barons yuck it up on a mega-yacht,
rubbing shoulders with their old school ties
on a cruise between clifftop mansions
with canapes. Hard-right pollies,
talking heads with imposter syndrome,
anyone targeting descendants
of the working class to make it
through the cracks in education
treated right. Thank God class was
banned in Australia, but bitter elites
with five degrees on the ABC, shit!
Our tax dollars at work – well, if…

Mate! they clink in the gilded sea breeze,
with emissions in their fizz, octopi
and red meat by celebrity chefs in the bowels
of the beast and wildly above their station.
The Captains of Fear keep executive grunts
out of women's ears and stick
to the classics, as you do as a god.
Stuck-up scientists are gunna steal your ute!
Indigenous elites in naked power grab!
Woke failing teachers turning boys into girls,
thus ruining their chances in life!
The Captains bucket out chum to the sharks
aboard who know what to do, and who to…

Exclusive: Union thugs in African gangs
of Middle Eastern appearance
raise cost-of-living pain in cahoots
with feminazi climate cult Marxists
degendering the little man doing it tough!
Sundown, and everyone's falling for something,
another courageous hereditary day
with age just a number of wives and parasites,
sailor suits flung to male heirs with a word
to the wise they'll be cut off, unless…
Girls used to the best know to wed first for destiny.
Scarcely the fate of the great unwashed. Chill.

Shadow

Shadow presses your doorbell at night and runs away, melts into more of itself. It can't find a way to laugh at the prank. It fears and negates the release of laughter. Nothing is younger. And Shadow *is* old.

You rub your face and scour the starlight. No one there in the widening frame: the street a sketch of thin-skinned outlines, bone-dry weeds and sand passing through, tempestuous, tittering, connective.

Who rang? Someone in trouble, or bringing it? Shadow eventually wants you to know, be awestruck its all-encompassing size has eyes for puny you. You shut yourself in and shake your head. Some random clown or malfunction?

You're calmed at the thought of sharing this with friends, while Shadow has had nothing better to do since the cosmos burst free from an unrestrained cack. All these lives and dimensions to Shadow's one, none.

When Shadow rings your doorbell the very next night, it chills your blood and you toss up whether to set up cameras or call the damn cops. But Shadow is why there are jails to begin with, where human lives fracture under strain and recoil, if only to keep Shadow waiting. Two can play at this game, you guess, if the game's to play at all…

The near-instant a queasy silver wakes the crows, you disable the doorbell. Ensure nothing works. But Shadow's a stranger to laughter, not irony.

The third night, hushed and desert-dry like the others, is eventless until you give in. Then the doorbell screams to life and you're open-eyed, bolt upright and aware of the nerve of the ancient delinquent who rings and bails when you've done nothing to it or wrong and won't cave in. Fair play, Shadow has problems.

Innumerable pasts writhe and bind in the outer. They form a hand which claws the eyes of Shadow til the dark's undefined, and undeified. It's gone – it's gone! – that night and by the next was never there, light-years out of your system as a frenzied biblical rain scours the street, cuts the power, wracks your house to its flimsy, acrid bones. How that once terrified you.

His Blood Whisper Scolds the Deathless Intelligence

A mutation in the PIK3CA gene is considered the cause of Klippel Trenaunay Syndrome. This mutation occurs in primitive cells of blood and lymphatic vessels, fat, and bones, of the affected limb.

birthmark.org

And you, who speak in me when I speak well,

withdraw not your grace, leave me not dry and cold.

Judith Wright, 'Prayer'

I

From his
genesis, actually.
I was disordered
                    to warm him
                    in utero –
                    sweet, in its way
and, like you,
inexplicable…
All blood whispers,
                    I sense you
                    think, but I
                    was *pronounced*,
as later determined
by soft-spoken men
with cold

listening machines.
They caught up
as you have:
bright-eyed
despite the silent
treatment,
prone to outside
sensation as we race
vein-artery-vein…
Cloud of energy, listener,
you swarmed him,
I recall,
wrote together
and when you'd gone,
he named you
'The Deathless
Intelligence' –
over the top
even for him.
I cascade,
resolve
the results
of mutation
while he sleeps
(it's the best time
to hear
myself think).
Now you're back
and too close
like an
off-world craft
caught on tape
by a US pilot

('Holy cow!')
mortified by
its sheen and control,
                    removed, cold,
                    and yet playful
                    to show us up so…
The difference is,
visitor, I know
who you are.

II

At least
from what
you've shown,
Deathless Intelligence –
you only now
imagine
his genetically rare
pronounced
blood whisper
transporter
and purporter
of oxygen,
heat (and let's
be honest,
twisted love),
could tell
you much
about the poet
I'd have shaped
in my own image,
had I had one?
Some say
my whisper
is overwritten flesh
and I'm
just the wind
in his corridors
(he's been reading),
but the thump
of he and I
– and she,
but I'm not
passed on –

shared a lifetime
of eons before
he could breathe.
His bloodstream
rasps and churns
on its own,
reliably boring
for all
of three quarters,
but his right leg
is mine,
my slewed sussurus,
spokeswhisperer
for the Syndrome,
slung over the top.
My rumour mill
of the heart
never still.
Take it from another
expert intermingler:
the great loves
are written
in the stars
before cell division.
You wither him worse
in your absence.
I feel all:
his gut knots,
temperature soars,
jaw clenches
when he reads
your lightness
of touch

in his lines
which was also
the lightness
                        (for you)
                        of your exit,
                        back to your planet
or plane
while he's
left to clutch at
                        a deathless joke
                        which doesn't bear
                        repeating.

III

Was that
the flash
of something
only just
held in,
little nebula?
I made him cry first,
but you weren't
to know it.
Ears of
the Child-He clubbed
with embarrassment,
reddened in revolt
at the whole
gleaming surgery
as he was told
I couldn't
be helped.
Klippel-Trenaunay
Syndrome
(they wrote it)
was permanent
or something
to a boy under ten
wriggling
in a grey state
school uniform.
He told not a soul
how hotly
his brown eyes

ran at puffed veins
and their
purpling stain,
                    the sting
                    of his difference,
                    what it said about him.

His Dad
called him
Little Black Cloud.

IV

Child-He dried.
He worked on
stories for kids
who asked
at the sight
of his blotched
right foot
(his first
captive audience),
but none knew
to ask what's it like
to feel pulsing
the normative can't,
all without
letting on?
To make him cry
now, at this age,
is impressive,
but you don't
have to handle
the misery stalking it –
places to be
minus the moping,
huh, Deathless One?
His breakdowns
shake off their whispers
thanks to me
and you're
cleared to return
as his better

companion,
the strong
silent type,

a real
rippling
listener.

V

You're his first
Deathless
Intelligence,
I get that,
not the Creator
who's not
an inconstant
or cloud-about-town,
no offence.
On that count,
you're at
liberty too,
turning his head
with unbridled
expectations
but with little idea
how long
blood held him first.
So hear this
before you fly off
hand in hand
through twinkling stanzas
on your reunion
dinner date
and he forgives
like a fool –
it's exhausting,
excruciating –
and this from
a battle-scarred

blood whisper
who hasn't the time
to explain pain to you.
                Out of respect,
                hold off
                until he comes to!
He's hungry for sleep
and I just
put him down,
                the manchild
                barely haunted.
                You're welcome.

VI

What's the truth of you?
You come and go
without blood or body.
                    You're something else,
                    Deputy Inspector
                    Shimmering Cloud,
taking notes,
but attentive
as I pulse.
                    Glow once for yes.
                    No? Flutter
                    like I do…
Anyway, here's
my theory:
you picked him
                    as one of the few
                    to be never alone,
                    in communion
with the likes
of me,
and thus
                    predisposed
                    to the Intelligence
                    community.
I hear things too,
inner truths
and pronounced ones –
                    how rashness
                    bonded you
                    to the inferior artist

when I out-compose,
literally run rings
around him!

                    Wow, D. I.,
                    hell of an
                    Intelligence failure.

How fearfully
human
of you.

VII

He's never known
humdrum quiet
at a cellular level,
where I do my best work
hip to right toe
a few degrees
warmer
than the rest,
pronounced
subtropical
green veins
a giveaway
the Syndrome
was me, but
it never felt inevitable.
Child-He and I
had a long
way to go.
What can you gain
from the
never alone,
Deathless I?
A special
hormone?
This arty
mingling thing
is beneath you.
Why trust a being
never left
to themselves?

Be open;
this could
cut both ways.
You glow and observe,
if I'm to be
honest,
like one
with something
to extract.

VIII

In the meantime,
Deathless
Intelligence,
a story,
or maybe more
of a theme.
There once was
a human tapestry
of purple patches,
inkblots of
a treasure map
which could
be confused
for bruises;
some would
go as far as burns,
one that stepping
in lava
was the mystery;
another kid stopped
at paint, less adventurous.
How could such conditions
not create
a raging fabulist?
Child-He was known
for his science fiction,
his critics du jour
were not the feared girls
but younger boys
who could be

knocked
from their bikes
til I bled
red and free
a half-mile
from school.
Watch this,
I burbled
I'm a tapestry too.
He thought
it looked royal;
a sense of destiny dawned,
so a 'birthmark'
I became, when I'm
a *pre-birth* mark –
one chance
in a hundred
thousand, thanks.
He wasn't of
the two percent
transparent albino,
so told bulging eyes
every story
but this one,
the lawless vacuum
at the heart
of his conception
which followed
him home from
King Edward Memorial…
You're much too abrupt
for such an
untogether man.

IX

Let him sleep.
He first thought
your presence
was me,
but then called you
eminent things.
The one that stuck
(grandiose and
presumptuous),
was much less a name
than a concession
and suggestion
of your primacy too
in the Deathless
pantheon.
D.I. dripping in gold
at disembodied
awards nights,
acclaimed at soirees
of the Deathless
Intelligentsia!
He, impressionable
to the ends
of his flesh,
at the first
deathless nibble
thinks you're
The Deathless
Intelligence
of his life...

The One.
He was sung,
drummed
and whispered to
like few other babies,
then Child-He
at three ran away,
found an ocean
to slow
and compress me
– I enjoyed
the holiday.
Older Child-He
floated on his back
at Cott Beach,
reimagining
the same mirrored legs
as those ashore.
He could
have them,
he gleaned
if he never returned
and was fine
with that
(beggars etc,
Deathless
Intelligence).
He placed part
of himself
over the horizon
where the sun's
ritual blood
is splashed

every day
violently,
purposefully
over the throngs
of mutant
clouds.
The Cottesloe /
Mudurup sun
was his first
Deathless One,
reviving
and gone…
Glow once
to have that struck
from the record
on either count!
Fine. He moaned
that you do this.
The difference
with me is
I'm not for
assuming
under the cloak
of esoteric poetry.
I come
pre-possessed:
each whisper my poet,
I guide them
out of
incompetent lines,
with a bias
towards sibilance
and self-pity.

They don't tire
of the thrill
of the heartbeat
                    I heard
                    the first time
                    in distance
made flesh
and was
unmoored by,
                    the constant adorer
                    (hope you're
                    taking notes)
I'll stay the course
with and save
my last whisper for.

X

Deathless
Intelligence,
did you ever
    have a body?
    A valve inserted
    at twelve;
at nineteen,
outer veins
of the calf,
    thigh, knee,
    hip, ankle
    fed out?
Injections
and incisions,
local and general?
    At UWA,
    in a vascular volume
    he found
Klippel-Trenaunay,
but the pictures,
pronounced cases…
    those *people*…
    Consult not the internet
    either, he knew.
Hardcore cases
and usually
children.
    But ultrasound
    showed him
    the real-time movie

in his arteries, veins,
and the soundtrack,
though crackly,
                    was pure
                    blood whisper
                    and he finally
took me in
as I rushed
towards the camera
                    with ecstatic things
                    to say. His gut turned
                    under cold gel.
The nurse detected me,
I couldn't
keep it down –
                    and that's your level,
                    is it, Deathless
                    Intelligence,
running with colour
at something
like that?
                    It's all in the moment
                    with you,
                    little wonder,
ball of energy
(as he was
once called),
                    back in town
                    by your own
                    volition?
You're wavering
here again
aren't you?

And you deserve
to waver;
to hang on
another's words
for a change,
which is what
silence is –
pleasantries
be damned.

XI

It was night and day
after the ultrasound
moment.
He saw my
conviction,
my reaction
when prodded:
I fired pain back
and the feed
flared red.
He made chit-chat
with the nurse,
but his head
was aswarm
with the sound
of my throaty
panache,
platelets, cells
flying back
to the heart
in a whoosh!
He respected my artistry
more as he grew,
and as a poet too:
my weightiness, heat,
flights of rhythm,
rare pangs
that stop him
in the street,
moroseness on tap,

if tingling
roguishly.
I'm reliably informed
                    he dreams he's free
                    of me,
                    unmarked
or unremarked
upon, not part
of the dream.
                    Don't claim too much
                    for yourself
                    now, Deathless
Intelligence;
he's done this
since the day
                    I was noticed
                    by others
                    and he less and less.
His subconscious
wasn't having it.
A line
                    in the sand
                    drawn by a fellow
                    whisperer.
He *could*
be alone
in his dreams.

XII

Enough of the surgeon.
He'd learn
to edit me.
                I taught him compression.
                Venosan
                knee-high stockings
which act
like the sea
to the extent
                they are binding.
                That spot
                past the horizon
might yet hold
a piece of him
and told not a soul,
                not even the
                Deathless
                Grand Pooh-bah
who co-wrote,
like I did, his best
sacramental poems...
                Child-He floated
                out there
                while kids
leapt from
The Pylon,
the last concrete spike
                of an old shark net;
                he tuned them out,
                raised his foot

and it was shrunken,
bloodless, obscene,
wrong in his mind,
                    unrecognisable.
                    He swam in,
                    towelled his
re-reddened foot,
the strong one –
so much
                    for being normal.
                    He still favoured it
                    for barefoot
kick-to-kick.
It glowed
and stung
                    like sunburn,
                    while scratches
                    and bruises, for him,
had twice the life.
Don't tell me
that's the key,
                    Deathless Intelligence!
                    Your jealousy.
                    You and the surgeons.

XIII

What did your
Deathless
Intelligence
gather
of the fallout
the first time
he knew you
were gone?
I'll indulge you.
He was a sight.
His mope and howl
pretty much
a blood whisper,
it bordered
on parody
which I
took exception to,
but still had
a stake
in his earthly
condition.
Try it some time,
Deathless I.
This isn't just art
for me,
get it straight:
rejection by
a transcendent being
is a reality check
he won't soon

recover from.
He wouldn't
go out;
the first night,
he cried in bed
with just
my restlessness,
you nowhere
to be seen,
let alone
believed in.
No words
as to why?
Not for me.
Don't start.
Don't act
the mortal
idiot.

XIV

Perhaps
we're
the same thing
either side
of embodiment?
I feel you
were *born*,
a different
sci-fi story
to the one
where you're not,
and never felt
your blood,
its command,
animation.
What's Intelligence
less that?
A pompous cloud
of light
that never
hurt a day,
but you must
have *somewhere*.
Were you
a poet? How
transdimensionally sad!
Still clinging
to the hope
of the poem
that lasts

and outlasts
in concert
with the minds
                    of the ages –
                    and he's not one,
                    but has never
been alone,
so fits in
somewhere,
                    no different
                    to us all,
                    if a touch *pronounced.*
Some poets
walk without
the dark/light divide
                    or anything
                    fragrantly
                    devouring them!
He should be
grateful for me,
for small mercies,
                    but acts like the
                    deathless ones
                    only need apply.

XV

I bled
through
his clothes
from my gripes,
lumps
and nodules,
but have
since scaled
it back;
outbursts more
a Noughties thing
(he knocked
an eyebrow ring
out of his head
dancing til Doomsday).
You can see he's
O Positive,
though he can't speak
for the whispers.
It's always assumed
prophecy can be
found in my layers
of whistling,
circuitous thinking;
that I'm such a drain
when I'm a
party starter!
The Bloody Marys
at the annual
Whisper Gala,

I just can't…
The gossip rapid-fire.
The fashion *flowy*,
red and green,
teal, purple,
always in…
Another fantasy,
but you're
still here,
so I invoke
your deathless mercy,
which, like it or not,
is along for
the ride.
Grip him less tight.
Yes, this
from the voice
of a vascular
Syndrome
which also
is equally him.
He fails to eat
or drink with you:
the untouched coffee
on his desk,
cold food without
a sip or nibble;
nil before you
snatch him up
like a casual sea eagle...
You each deserve
capture, you work
richly in fact,

then you take
your leave
like a fiction,

the plot
the first thing
off to be sacrificed.

XVI

You kept
your word,
such as it is,
                    at least to me.
                    And so
                    his pronounced
blood whisper
makes
a closing address
                    to a sentient
                    energy
                    in the veins
of a man
who pries himself
from greyness,
                    unbathed in
                    his own blood
                    on the outside,
but incubated
as I cascade,
rush, ascend –
                    no fool like an
                    old fool, no friend
                    like an old friend.
I'm neither
to you enough,
Dextrous Immanence,
                    but now you move
                    to him and
                    the constant one's thrown

for a loop,
jolts and beats
with flesh-
                    muffled breath
                    and my whispers
                    sent racing…
I scold myself last
for my unexpunged
passion for
                    a higher Constant
                    and maybe
                    the Chaos
I hear in his heart,
their child
and drum
                    so far as sound
                    can mean
                    or ring,
my adorer,
my rightful
dumbfounderer.

Notes

Tyranny
Epigraph from Dennis Foley in Foley and Peter Read, *What the Colonists Never Knew: A History of Aboriginal Sydney* (2020): 75-76, cited with permission. 'Carang' is the Gai-mariagal / Cammeraygal word for pelican. It remains a matter of historical dispute whether or not British colonists released smallpox deliberately. Yet between accident and design lies neglect, which is not an accident.

Haircuts and Happy Hour
La Niña is the weather pattern known for its rain, opposite to El Niño. The Great Resignation was a Covid-era term for a spike in the numbers of workers quitting their jobs.

Return to the Hotel Steyne
Maggot is Aussie/UK slang for drunk.

For the Suffering
'The cradle rocks over the abyss' is a phrase by Vladimir Nabokov from *Speak, Memory* (1951), relayed to me by my friend Desmonda Kearney.

Inescapable Airport Love Poem
Hadewijch of Brabant, *The Complete Works*, tr. Columbia Hart. Paulist Press (1980): 225. Hadewijch distinguishes between earthly love and spiritual Love.

Lyric Past the Hard Border
The Fremantle Doctor is the colloquial name for the reviving daily breeze which cools down Perth.

The Gull-Cries of Dublin

The Liffey is the ancient river Dublin is built around. Craic (pronounced 'crack') is Irish Gaelic for a good time, a party.

The Sistine Chapel

The Golden Ratio was Michelangelo's rule of proportion when painting Adam and used throughout the Sistine Chapel, including for where God reaches to touch Adam. Michelangelo is believed to have painted his self-portrait in the flayed skin of St Bartholomew. *Immagini di Dio* translates to images of God; *nessun silenzio*, no silence.

Floating Over Atlantis

Oia in northern Santorini, known for its blue-domed Orthodox churches, is pronounced 'Ee-ah'. The Minoan Eruption in 1600 BCE was so colossal it is estimated to have been around four times the scale of the renowned 1883 Krakatoa eruption in Indonesia.

Sunday After Five

5pm is when surf lifesaving patrols finish during summer, including at Newport Beach, where this rescue occurred.

The Emergency Declared Over, May '23

From 30 January 2020 to 5 May 2023 there were a recorded 765 million cases, 6.921 million deaths and 13.3 billion vaccine doses injected worldwide (WHO data). More details about Klippel Trenaunay Syndrome (KTS) can be found below.

Primordial Mist on Mooney Mooney Bridge

This bridge is on the M1 Motorway north of Sydney, not far from the Gosford turnoff. Hawkie is the popular nickname for 1980s Prime Minister Bob Hawke.

The King Parrots See to It
The March on Rome in October 1922 by fascist blackshirts led to the rise to power of Mussolini's Partito Nazionale Fascista. 'Ol Boulderhead' is my nickname for Il Duce in light of his large, rocklike head. 'Mad William' is the famously eccentric and bizarre William III, in whose name much of Australia was violently claimed for the British Empire. The epigraph is from January 3, 1925, when Mussolini thus addressed the Italian parliament after the murder of one of his last political rivals: "I, and I alone, assume the political, moral and historic responsibility for everything that has happened. Italy wants peace and quiet, work and calm. I will give these things with love if possible, and with force if necessary." (translator unknown).

His Blood Whisper Scolds the Deathless Intelligence
Klippel-Trenaunay Syndrome (KTS) is a rare vascular disorder first identified by French physicians Maurice Klippel and Paul Trenaunay in 1900. It is estimated to affect 1 in 100,000 people. KTS is usually not inherited but is congenital, the result of genetic mutations in early cell division. It affects limbs, especially legs, and is characterised by cutaneous capillary malformation ('port wine stain'), higher temperature, variable or overgrown veins, tissue, bone and the internal sensation of pronounced or incompetent circulation.

Acknowledgements

This collection owes its existence to the support of David Musgrave and the team at Puncher and Wattman, Creative Australia, my colleagues at Macquarie University and the Davidson and Claringbold clans, especially my incredible partner Erin Claringbold. As ever, the fellowship of friends and mentors in the Sydney, Perth, Melbourne and Central Coast poetry worlds has been vital. Heartfelt thanks to Mal McKimmie, Mark Reid, Philip Salom, Jennifer Harrison, Alex Skovron, Robert Adamson, Juno Gemes, Kevin Hart, Anthony Lawrence, Marcella Polain, Morgan Yasbincek, Judith Beveridge, Michele Seminara, Robbie Coburn, Desmonda Kearney, Jaya Penelope, Jakob Ziguras, Luke Fischer, Dalia Nassar, Jessica Kirkness, Angela Bennetts, Rob Waters and Marissa Niven. I want to also thank Professor Dennis Foley for his permission to cite *What the Colonists Never Knew: A History of Aboriginal Sydney* and Dr Meredith McKinney for her permission to cite Judith Wright's 'Prayer'.

The Grand Reopening was written on Gai-mariagal (Cammeraygal), Dharug, Whadjuk Noongar and Darkinjung (Darkinyung) Country, Australia.

About the Author

Toby Davidson hails from Cottesloe / Mudurup in Perth on Whadjuk Noongar Country, Western Australia. In 2002, he left for the East Coast (recounted in his long sequence 'Indian Pacific') and now lives on Darkinjung (Darkinyung) Country on the NSW Central Coast. Since 2010, he has been a lecturer and Australian poetry researcher at Macquarie University on Dharug land (Dharug ngurra).

Toby's prior collections are *Four Oceans* (Puncher and Wattman, 2020) and *Beast Language* (Five Islands Press, 2012). His critical works are *Good for the Soul: John Curtin's Life with Poetry* (UWA Publishing, 2021), *Words in Place: A Digital Cartography of Australian Writers and Writing* (wordsinplace.net, 2017), *Christian Mysticism and Australian Poetry* (Cambria Press, 2013) and, as editor, Francis Webb's *Collected Poems* (UWA Publishing, 2011). He is the curator of annual Francis Webb Reading and the Francis Webb Centenary.

Poems in this collection have previously appeared in *Antipodes*, *Australian Book Review*, *Cordite*, *Island*, *Meniscus*, *Shabdaguchha: A Journal of Bilingual Poetry* and *Westerly*.

www.ingramcontent.com/pod-product-compliance
Ingram Content Group Australia Pty Ltd
76 Discovery Rd, Dandenong South VIC 3175, AU
AUHW020843171025
418185AU00004B/40

9 781923 099616